The Invention of Secrecy

David Citino

The Invention of Secrecy

Ohio State University Press

Columbus

Library of Congress Cataloging-in-Publication Data
Citino, David, 1947–
    The invention of secrecy / David Citino.
      p. cm.
    ISBN 0-8142-0863-0 (alk. paper) —
    ISBN 0-8142-5066-1 (pbk. : alk. paper)
    I. Title
  PS3553.I86 I5 2001
  811'.54—dc21   00-047869

Text design by Diane Gleba Hall.
Jacket design by David Drummond.
Type set in Bembo by Tseng Information Systems.
Printed by McNaughton & Gunn.

The paper used in this publication meets the minimum requirements of the
American National Standard for Information Sciences—Permanence of Paper for
Printed Library Materials. ANSI Z39.48-1992.

9 8 7 6 5 4 3 2 1

Acknowledgments

I wish to thank the editors and readers of the following publications, in which these poems first appeared.

American Literary Review: "And So"

Anthology of Magazine Verse and Yearbook of American Poetry, 1997: "The Third Day of the Televised War, I Watch a Spider Walk across a Map of the World"

The Antioch Review: "Lady Di and Gianni Versace in Stores in Time for the Holidays"

Beloit Poetry Journal: "Naming the Grandmother" (reprinted in *Poetry Daily,* on-line)

Buon Giorno Magazine: "Hotel Bar, Winter, the Middle of Pennsylvania, with Mario Lanza"

The Centennial Review: "After the Poetry Festival," "Quattrocento Angels over Cleveland," "Stregone"

Cimarron Review: "Cycladic Island Female Statue, British Museum"

Connecticut Review: "Saying the Cold"

Defined Providence: "A Natural History of Shadows"

The Kenyon Review: "Walking the Mall"

Laurel Review: "Fossil Baby Found," "Hale-Bopp Comes to Ohio"

The Literary Review: "Shoes"

Mid-American Review: "The Discipline of Brick, the Sexuality of Corn"

My Bug: True Tales of the Car That Defined a Generation (Artisan): "Orange Beetle"

National Forum: "Fifty-two New Dead Sons of Rameses, One Hundred Thousand New Galaxies"

Nebraska Review: "At the Close of the Twentieth Century"

New Letters: "Famine" (reprinted in *Spud Songs*), "Tarantella"

Nightsun: "The Dig"

Ohio Review: "The Beatification of Padre Pio," "The Puncture"

Pleiades: "Visiting Writer, Days Inn"

Poetry: "The Invention of Secrecy"
Poetry East: "Hair"
River City Review: "Fecal Fossil Found," "Obsession"
Salmagundi: "The Dancing of the Underwear"
Shenandoah: "A Personal History of Sound, with Locomotive, Stage Murmurs, a Little Latin, a Little Sex"
Southern Humanities Review: "Folding Caravaggio," "The Man Who Found a Poem in Everything"
The Southern Review: "Dead Man Revives in Morgue," "Sky Burial"
VIA: Voices in Italian Americana: "Italian Couple Exposed in Photo-Booth Tryst"
West Branch: "Emperor Vespasian Cuts Off His Nose to Spite His Face"
Wind: "Horses"
Witness: "The Harrowing of Hell," "Homage to the Birds," "Working"

For Mildred Citino and Mary Hicks

Contents

III. Quattrocento Angels over Cleveland

IV. Walking the Mall

I. At the Close of the Twentieth Century

Hale-Bopp Comes to Ohio

It's 5 A.M., a pristine time for me
ever since the days I delivered
the *Plain Dealer* before Mass.

Star-headed romantic, I'd see
the face of the dreamy girl
I was "going steady with" glowing

in the clouds over Cleveland
as I left tracks across the dewy lawns,
bringing the citizens their bad news.

I had a girl, Donna was her name.
Since she left me, I've never been the same.
Old now, thick plastic between my eyes

and the cosmos, still I thrill to the end
of yesterday, morning's cleansing
of everything that used to be.

I pad through the dark house, brew
espresso, tinker with my little songs.
I walk out, look over the dark grass

to the neighbor's shagbark hickory.
And there it sits. Bigger than any star,
perched just beneath an upper branch—

rock, sludge, snow that seems to blaze
with fires that lit the dawn of time,
a comet from the moment before light.

What have you come to tell, messenger—
that by your next visit we all
will be stone and root and rank earth,

our heirs standing higher on our bones?
We did not need you to know where
we're bound. Still, I look at you

with something like awe. Never
have I seen my own going so radiant,
the sky lightening, the beauty of my death

twisting slowly its long, glittering tail.

Homage to the Birds

Who needs angels, with their smug *Oh but* we've *never fallen,* the officious carrying out of dark sentence and plague on behalf of the party in power, frightful annunciations and denunciations, sabre rattling, jawboning, the holier-than-thou carping along with the Father-always-liked-us-better smirk. They don't have to haul around flesh and bone, contend with misfiring neurons, tumors big as tennis balls, hearts fat and easily startled, the awful bind and ease of too much bad fruit. What hint do they have of the gravity of our lives? Archangels. Dominions. Thrones. They can't even get inside one another. Their job is to bar us from gardens, scare the hell out, do the police. Birds, on the other hand, have been brothers and sisters to us for eons, trying by day to make our thoughts, by night our dreams, a few notes lighter, sweeter, buffeted as we are by variable winds. Our passion and labor become grand opera in the airy twittering of their communion with dawn and dusk. Together so long, we've grown alike. While angels can adore one thing only, over and over, for ever and ever Amen, the birds, like us, try to put their fear and want to song. Most birds, before sexual maturity, learn from older singers of the tribe, father usually, though redwings steal a few notes from the territory of neighbors and work these in. Some, starlings for example, copy pieces of songs of other species. Some even add to their song news of the world, bark and yowl of cat and dog, clank of machinery, freeway whine and blat and honk, even our own human whistling. The more notes in a repertoire, the more successful the singer, fending off rivals, hovering with steady wings over a mate. *Hosanna! Praise! Praise!,* the angels sing, stuck in a groove of unceasing, unwarped adoration, utterly predictable. Birds are the real messengers, the true singers, their few notes taken from mother and father but made their own, lifting up among the faint stars to hold off darkness an hour or two longer, a music fitting like skin, wind riffling feathers, near as a name, their songs, entering our human lives—no matter how many times we hear—as startling as the flight, out of the body, of the body.

The Harrowing of Hell

I've heard it said that the fires
of hell had to be invented
by believers from southern climes;
northerners would fear only
chilblains, blood of barefoot ice.

Now not even Southern Baptists
take hell seriously. If we had to
invent it over again? Maybe
an unending series of phone calls
from MasterCard

we'd be obliged to answer
during heights of food or love,
marathon spiels by Allstate men
and Nissan dealers who knew
the kids' names. Days

of long papered tables
we knew already the minutes to.
Car chases. Kabooms. Special effects.
Zany, madcap sitcom mix-ups,
the grand laugh tracks of America

for ever and ever, Amen.
Or worse, tired ravings of racists,
jock-itch sexists, misanthropes,
the Ohio Unorganized Militia
certain they've cracked Revelation,

common law, Constitution.
Eternal whine, trying to blame
someone for what we think is pain.
Lyrics each generation thinks
it invented. No, the world won't

end in fire. No mention
in the Bible of purgatory. Not much
of hell. In the twelfth century
it blazed up like a damn fine idea.
And probably not ice. There's ease

in the numb drifting of millennia.
The real horror? I'd vote for
a small room of old salt and bone,
the thoughts of one mind, lukewarm,
too intent, too alone.

A Natural History of Shadows

Dawn. We're drawn into a world
of wall and lawn, to walk beside
our somber, charcoal companions.

Silent as wish or dread, they go
with us into the bright foreign land
where all appearance is certain,

dream remnants sewn into the image
Mother and Father cast earthward,
the dazzling erotic of their morning.

Noon's none too soon. Have we ever
been brighter? The newest orphans,
our fine friends missing in fire.

Now light itself begins to fail us,
shadows born again, moving
to our other side, imprecisions

of memory. At last we assume
the position, a field beneath
eloquent stone. A shadow rises

at our feet, the smoke of a life,
free of our limitations,
reaching for the nighest stars.

Fossil Baby Found

How deep, these dark eyes. Skull of smiling baby,
australopithecine infant, millions of years old,

no bigger than heads of the ones I helped lift
from the womb's sweet brew, but here, above the eyes,

two holes punched through whisper a nightmare flight
to a nest of African eagles. Knowing too little

to be sapiens, we were being schooled in our fear,
the attack stark and sharp but soft as mother's kiss

through soughing leaves, lethal talons slipping in.
A scream splits my own skull as my child is jerked up

suddenly to rush toward the sun, a mad thrash, prints
of the raptor marking her forever as a member

of our tribe. Prey a shade too slow, so caught up
in ourselves we can't dream we're not immortal, beasts

too rapt in things of the earth to keep an eye
to the sky, the fierce bird fixing us, biding his time,

then, racing toward us along the ground, a shadow.

Fifty-two New Dead Sons of Rameses,
One Hundred Thousand New Galaxies

Knowledge comes at us fast, and—
as when the catcher fires back hard
to the cocky pitcher still jawing toward
the visitor's dugout because earlier
he'd blown on his extended finger after
whiffing their gold-chained DH
and the bench was on him—it hurts.

In the Valley of the Kings, just found,
a vast burial, an Olympic stadium
carved out of the underworld. Lifetimes
of laborers—descendants of those who cut
the rock with blunt chisels—it will take,
and archaeologists lusting for tenure,
to make it through these doom rooms.

A week later we look up, having aimed
the Hubble with its Coke-bottle specs
toward Ursa Major, and there, out
beyond the dipper, a space between stars
with more space than we can imagine,
alight with new fires of spun, flung blood,
as if we saw inside to the very spurt of us.

These sightings below and above put us
in our place, reckon us caught
without visa between states of relic and star,
frozen between bases with the pitcher
running toward us, stony bone the only proof
of flesh, tiny rooms the light can't enter.
A blow to the head, this learning.

The Dig

Back of the old garage, odorous with
tires, gas, and creosote, where
compost pile and trash have stood
above posed, grinning skeletons

of pets—Princess, Bubba, Shadow,
and the rest—as long as anyone
can recall, we lay the grid, seeking

to turn up what we can about a place,
hold in today's hands the heft
of descent, each bleached bone.
Rising to the trench our shovels cut,

bottles holding last breaths
of the last to drink, newsprint stained
with scandals and ads, arrowheads,

earth black with ash and menstrual blood
of ruddy folk who fasted, feasted
under stars before the light
reached us, potsherds dark with grease,

priestly marks, hunters' teeth
and lovers'. Our poles break through
into monumental space. More stone,

and large jars of writings
so familiar we can't read ourselves
in any poem or tale, women and men
who loved their deaths enough

to save them for us under stone,
sarcophagi shattered by robbers,
we surmise, soon after the gods' children

were sealed in their little boats
to ride these earthen currents.
Lastly, poise of antlered dancers—
the hunt the one rite we need.

It's our provenience, this dirt
we've come from, enriched and fouled—
though you may not believe a word

of this, because, you could say,
I'm fooled by the way one story
of how we rose to this unmindful height
covers, hides light from the next;

but I know what I've told you
is beyond deceit, because we lust
for stories of what lies beneath,

and because belief will always be
our sentence for the crime of thinking
ourselves a tribe now and forever,
living but cursed with the itch to dig.

Emperor Vespasian Cuts Off
His Nose to Spite His Face

We spend such sweat
trying not to smell,
though love makes scents

to us. *Pecunia non olet,*
Vespasian is said
to have said when advised

it wasn't seemly to tax
Rome's public toilets,
Money doesn't stink.

Oh no? Take a whiff,
the rank miasma,
a fetid wind scouring

the earth, this carnal,
mortal business
everywhere you step,

steaming ash and waste,
the slaughterhouse,
the countinghouse,

even the seas made awful.
You think, you think
money doesn't stink?

Famine

All over Ireland, survivors held wakes
to keen away the departing, swoll-bellied specters

boarding black ships bound for hell or America.
You can't blame the potato, root-fruit

swaddled in rags, grimacing mug of tough kid
shoved hard in dirt. Landowners, whose law

forbade even the gathering of the manor's twigs
for a fire, flung it at the peasants, swill

for the troughs. When it rotted under fields
into plague's stink, the poor understood,

as they sometimes do, they'd asked too little,
waited a potato too long, prayed a day too hard.

The Third Day of the Televised War, I Watch
a Spider Walk across a Map of the World

A nation stares at itself
making cheap talk, war.
Newsreaders with great suits,
lips and breasts to die for.
How we like to watch.

Fly-boys blink frontier eyes.
Civilized bombs knock
and go in the front door.
Say hello to Allah, Iraqi soldier!
A boffo success, this war.

It's not that once we were
less cruel. We've bathed in gore
since night was the cave.
But how can we now
not think war a fraud?

A televised *Victory at Sea*
brought my father back
from the stench of Guadalcanal.
His world war sired me.
And I'm powerless to stop this.

Feeling I'm being watched,
I look up to startle
at the intruder, a dark hunter
stalking across the world
hanging from the wall.

I feel it, insidious shiver,
cold of tooth and bone.
The victim caught, struggling,
a noiseless scream. Again,
again there is no reason.

At the Close of the Twentieth Century

These are the days—the heels
of running gunmen clicking

on concrete in parking garages,
monsters who mean business

menacing kids in dark stairwells,
only the shouters and howlers

being heard above the brute din
of days, birds falling from the sky

as if to signify the very end
of things—we envy the trees.

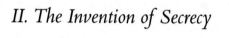

II. The Invention of Secrecy

The Invention of Secrecy

The ancients were not able, save
for a few remarkable ones —
Alexander, Julius Caesar, Ambrose —

to read, or write, silently. *I would
have written to you sooner,* Cicero wrote
to a friend, *but I had a sore throat.*

Read to yourself, we say to children
still today. This they cannot do.
Saying the Latin answers at the Mass,

dressed in my white Sears shirt under
medieval cassock and surplice,
Chuck Taylor Converse All-Stars —

to protect the sacristy carpet —
I heard some new music. The words
tasted nothing like Cleveland.

Ages ago, library, school, temple
were loud places where tongues flexed,
heart and lungs giving, taking,

the song and dance of subduing self
enough to put in our mouths words
of another body, words of our own.

Learning to read without even moving
our lips, we invented private life.
We created secrets of the dark hollows

of bone and flesh, a new selfishness,
deceiving ourselves into believing
that, alone, we could be complete,

silent, we would not grow too full.

And So

                your mother died
just hours ago, you called to say,
rather than write—because you know
we're tempted to believe nothing happens
off the page—and your two brothers
had been furloughed from the pen
to be by her side, even the one
who'd been let off death row
by the liberal governor from Yale.

And so this brother, the murderer
I mean, had cursed you and taken
your keys because when she lay down
on what we knew was her deathbed,
you fell hard off the wagon after
three good years as her nurse
through the radiation and chemo
because you couldn't imagine life
without such a death to prepare for.

And so you promise me you'll detox
and go back to A.A.—
either the one that still remembers
your father, who back
in his Kentucky hollow would shoot
at flies in the living room with his .38
while you kids shook in your beds,
whose gun your mother would hide
in the oven, or the gay A.A. near campus.

And so you called, weeping,
to tell me this because you know
of the compulsion we share to write
what we can't stop losing,
and writing it would please her,
if one out of the pain of this world
can know joy beyond escaping,
and because in this room of books
where so little news of the world gets in,

we would talk, about poems, together.

The Man Who Found a Poem in Everything

Haunted—the creaky mansion
of his childhood. Shades
of bloodsuckers and saints,
drafty stanzas furnished
with the careworn and threadbare:

beribboned khaki rags
Daddy wore to conquer Japan,
stamps from perforated lands,
Slovakia, Danzig, Fascist Italy,
first baseman's mitt damp

with neat's-foot oil, photo
of the one who each red dawn
died in Latin and returned
at night, autographed *Sincerely,*
Savior of the Living Dead.

He learned to throw his voice,
had a knack for finding words
he felt he had to say
under someone else's tongue.
His every line? Made to be broken.

Not yet metered out, breath
was unruly. He couldn't speak
without repeating himself
but began to find something salty
in the bite of every sentence.

His parents grew from wisps,
chemicals fuming in maelstroms
of Big Bang, blood-bitter spumes
of primal sea, to lungfish
beaten ashore by tides, then

mammals biding their time in trees
for dark to spirit away the dinosaurs.
At last he made them myths:
power-mad Dad gunning the engine,
shouting he'd have things *his* way

by God, and Mom wreathing hair
into snakes writhing wildly. Guilt
spotted his pants when anyone
in her image and likeness smiled
demurely and crossed her legs.

A young woman barged in, gave
herself in limber, inspired ways
in his parents' massive bed at night,
yet in revision he insisted
she was unattainable utterly.

He shattered her into images,
hips rounded like sea-heaves
to bear creation once again
and recapitulate phylogeny,
nipples engorged, taut at his lips,

their heaving together a fading
of borders that unmixed
his metaphors. It was her art
that knitted tiny bones that set
souls to flying. They named names.

His mind the deafening scratch
of pen on paper, but the truth is
he was running out of things
to unforget. Those near him
heard music soft as the bell

at the end of the typed line
or *tick* of broken pencil point.
Without words at last,
he'd learned to make an eternity
of the silence of his name.

Visiting Writer, Days Inn

I think I'm being pulled out of my life, static
of Blood-of-the-Lamb radio waxing, waning
the Alleghenies, wakes of careening big rigs—
passing words blurred—but I catch up with myself

three crow-loud carrion deer, two rank rest stops
later. I'm a name printed on spines of thin books,
scrawled on the card at the front desk. *Here
on business, sir? I'm the writer,* I reply, coloring

at the small evasion. The clothes I hang are effigies
breathing out a signature, shock of familial clouds,
and more intimacy, poems I lift from suitcase
along with razor—ways of marking days.

Dinner at the *Scotch & Sirloin.* What do they expect
from the poet their money brought here, prints
stamped madly in pristine snow? I behave.
The new dean in a new suit still fears the old,

trumpets himself, the deathlessness of poems,
intones to the table, *But at my back I
always hear Time's wingéd chariot hurrying near.*
We toast Poetry. We eat some. We toast Poetry.

It's time, the hall full as it will get, and it
comes back, that nearly unafraid attention
to be paid, the trying to say, time after time,
That is to say. It's what I do. At dawn tomorrow,

students looking through me as they resume
their lives, my eyes red, I'll climb back into
time's chariot, nurse two bad tires all the way
to Ohio, inn of those days I always never leave.

After the Poetry Festival

All had seemed safe here,
a universe of ivied buildings,
white colonial, earnest kids
of the American upper middle class
on their way to junior vice-president
or Princeton. The Alleghenies
ran like whales breaching
the profound blue, the Susquehanna
floating the Republic beyond danger.

But as I head west on I-80,
it leaks into the car,
the fading, rising static. Bad news.
I wonder for the first time
this weekend, what happens when
the poem ends? Can I make it home
from here? *Immune system deficiencies* . . .
Bruised, battered mother, child . . .
A tanker leaking toxins . . .

A big rig rips by, rocking me
so suddenly I don't know at first
I'm not flying, and then stars
strewn low along the road—but no,
not stars: the eyes of numberless deer
waiting to cross the interstate,
man's dark and deadly road,
jewels fixed in my high beams,
giving my light back to me.

At dawn, orange-clad hunters
will infiltrate these woods.
Carrion, the great teacher,
will bring its stinking lessons,
news on the hour. But now
what I carry is some pure hope.
All the way to Ohio, my eyes tear
with what I've seen and heard,
with what the deer know.

The Discipline of Brick, the Sexuality of Corn

Months now I've watched
the masons brick the walls
of the grand new building
near my own, a ritual

of breath, eye, and hand
that takes the light away
one story at a time.

Each hard-edged instant
succumbs to the next until
a line is drawn precisely
parallel to this earth,

fire-tried sentences
scaling four horizons
of horse chestnut, maple, oak.

And corn in the fields
as I go home each day,
one hundred thousand tassels
having appeared one dawn

through wisps of Ohio mist,
gold flames flickering
above tiers of waving arms,

like childhood illustrations
of Pentecost, inspirations
that burn the tongue.
This is how a life is made.

Walls grow from side to side
and on up to the roof
to begin their slow erosion,

the rank and file stand
to dance before the harvester—
the mortal satisfaction
of again and again.

Working

1. The Writer

When we'd walk our paychecks over to Danny's
each Friday at noon for pierogi (6 kraut, 6 potato)
brown with buttered onion, fishbowls of Stroh's

so wet and cold they'd turn the hand to stone,
and a neat little stack of bills—one crisp hundred,
some tens, twenties, change—we'd never laugh

when Edison, of Logan, West (By God!) Virginia—
who'd left school in fourth grade because
of Daddy's black lung and come to Cleveland

needing work—turned his check over on the bar
and in front of Danny made his large, careful *X*.
Back at work after the heavy meal, one beer

too many and some nine-ball, feeling my wallet
fatter now and tightening my jeans, I'd look
at the job I'd just done as if it told me

something about myself not even Jesus knew,
reach into the tool apron around my hips
for the grease pencil, and sign my initials

on the sweat-stained Completed Work card
with a special dance of the hand, the machines
all around, loud enemies just that morning,

humming and throbbing something sweet
about the weekend, a girl, a pink Ford convertible,
and seeming (I know you'll laugh at this)

almost beautiful.

2. The Shame

They called me Professor because I had dreams
of college someday. Summers so hot
you couldn't get hard standing against the table

no matter what she was doing to you inside
your head, the metal would stick to your skin,
and it was treated, so not even the deep cuts

would heal. The fiberglass though was worse.
It seemed to work its way under the flesh.
Keep your goddamn hands off my wife,

the big drunk, just arrived at the Wonder Bar,
said to me. Egged on by the crazy brothers
whose bullying of those younger or smaller

was the quick sucker punch to the balls or what
they called the titty twister—they'd not let go until,
through the blue-bruising, siren pain, you whistled—

I'd walked over, asked, "You want to dance?"
"Almost Persuaded" by David Houston, I recall,
or maybe "He'll Have to Go," Jim Reeves.

As pretty as her smile as she said yes, I hear
more clearly today his hissing rasp and the laughter
at our beery table as I returned red-faced, head down.

There was a fight later that night, but I went out
into the head-clearing city air, fists unscarred
because I knew that at dawn I had to be at work,

drill in my fist, punching the metal again and again.

III. Quattrocento Angels over Cleveland

Italian Couple Exposed in Photo-Booth Tryst

Caught *in flagrante,* stowing away
in steerage, a do-it-yourself love boat.

Privacy is hard to come by. Lovers
need to find new ways to say *So long.*

They had an hour before his sad train
withdrew from the terminal,

leaving her unsatisfied in the way
only one left bereft on the brink can be.

They'd have gotten away with it
had their passion not pounded, rocked

the booth, shaking the curtain, two actors
fumbling for the same grand entrance,

as tourists and commuters thronging
in the Genoa train station swelled

to an audience outside the hot-flashing
Bower of Bliss. We can't be content

with the art of being human in the dark,
our grand dance. We need to make

acts of art of the very acts of life,
so that later—in the tranquillity

we're doomed as humans to undergo
for long spells, or briefly every now

and then—we can know what it is
not to be silent, cold, alone.

Lady Di and Gianni Versace in Stores
in Time for the Holidays

In Napoli, craftsmen work overtime
        on sainthood, figuring our devotion
with painstaking, Old World hands.

The Bambino, his Mother, of course,
        and a few others miraculously constant
in the fitfully fervid South: Sts. Nicola,

Francesco, Antonio di Padova, and rows
        and rows of angels swathed in dimpled folds
of precious fat. As human time passes,

mischance assumes others into our dreams.
        Two saints newly canonized in terra cotta.
Princess Di (Santa Bulimia) and Gianni Versace

of Calabria and Miami Beach (St. Cool),
        tinctured in blue and gold to catch flickers
flung from vigil lights, faces bright and pure

as snow in photos in glossy magazines.
        O, Diana, pray for us, the loathing we hold
for our own common days. Gianni, nobody

in heaven looks better. Teach us
        how mortal life can seem outside the flash
of fame, how frail we feel unclothed.

Folding Caravaggio

A Mafia turncoat told an Italian court that a long-lost Caravaggio
had been destroyed 30 years ago.
    REUTERS

A man can stumble early in a broken land
into the old ways of power. A man thinks
he must bend things his way, his way

the power to crease the very things
that are beautiful only if unbroken—
my shame. I am the *pentito,* turncoat,

reciting the tale no one wishes to believe.
The *Nativity* hung for ages in the Oratorio
of San Lorenzo in Palermo, until

that night, the frightening stars falling
on the pale baby and Virgin, forcing her
on her knees so soon after delivery,

to pose, muscled beasts, angels leaning in
to hosanna demands for submission,
near enough to touch her. I knifed it out,

this miracle used to explain all others,
folded it to get past the guard, and later,
unfolding, saw the harm it does,

this trying to rise above one's nature
or neighborhood, the wish to manhandle
the white thighs of eternal beauty.

The paint flaked away like dirty snow,
feathers of a wounded bird. When
the buyer saw, he broke into sobs, ran

out of the room. I know I'll suffer for all
the bad I've made with these heavy hands.
All my life I did what I was told.

A good soldier. Like that little girl.
There's no quitting the organization,
they've told me time and again. She

must have known it too. Now I'm
my own man. Soon enough I'll sleep
with the fishes. See to it my daughter,

weeping now outside my cell, is kept
from harm. May her beauty not
cause the eye of God to fall on her.

The Dancing of the Underwear

A village mayor in northeast Italy has banned people living near the local church from hanging out their underwear to dry on balconies, saying it was time for some civic decency.
REUTERS

For weeks and weeks, secret meetings,
heated doorway hissings back and forth,
hands frantic in the air at market,
in *trattoria,* the very church.

Perspiring but dazzlingly formal
in scarlet sash and his best hat,
he addresses those assembled, a modest
but resolute legion of decency.

Certain families—I won't say which—
are without shame, without honor,
the mayor of Pieve di Curtarolo
intones as the *paparazzi,* who came

all the way from Florence and Rome,
scratch behind their notebooks.
Isn't it time, citizens, to put on
the vestments of respectability

Italy has forever been known for?
But men playing cards on the square
know better, women and girls making
the sweet *passeggiata,* cool evening

whispering beneath their skirts.
They understand their Italy means
this weekly miracle, the resurrection,
fresh and sweet, of the underwear.

They worship the slim ghostly *donna*
ashimmy in the slightest breeze,
walking wanton in wind beside
her graceful, dashing *cavaliere.*

True lovers recognize the shape
of desire, love's mortal form.
They can see that such display—
cotton and silk dazzling in noon,

bulge, swell, thrust, and yield,
the waft of bodies dancing
the parts of a woman and a man—
is ever and always beyond shame.

Stregone

Magic Potion Kills Sicilian Fisherman
    REUTERS

The corpse of unlucky Luigi,
hued a deep blue and aglow
in the morgue's morbid dark,
summoned first the doctors

and then the carabinieri,
who stood around the body,
heads uncovered, mouths agape,
and crossed themselves.

The Italian South: such things
do happen. A fisherman, beset
by evil spirits that had plagued
his family and their boat

for years, visits the *stregone,*
the sorcerer, who uses
the natural world to placate Fate.
There is no power like belief.

My own great-grandfather
was the magus of his village.
He knew, no matter how dark
things got, how cursed the luck,

just what to say or brew.
For every pig or peasant
in stony Serrastretta
sick of body, mind, or soul,

he knew a root, song, poem.
But his powers were stolen
by a young doctor from Naples
who poisoned the old man's flock

one moonless mountain night
to prove his potions more potent.
Time arrests every mystery
but the one last act.

The *stregone* who changed
Luigi's luck for good is charged
with murder, second degree.
O Great-Grandfather, Bisnonno,

say something wise. My brain
glows on the MRI screen
bright as poor Luigi, provinces
of the body in hot revolt.

I feel bad for the doctors,
who, shuffling paper, can think
of no good song for me.
I could almost believe

in the olden ways, days
of childhood mystery and awe,
when most of us had the luck
to be perfectly whole

of mind and soul, good angels
could outfight the bad,
and there was, for each disease,
one herb, a few good words.

Hotel Bar, Winter, the Middle of
Pennsylvania, with Mario Lanza

Always you could catch me
off guard with the brute youth
of that voice. Not sure what
I'm doing here, a *faux* Amish hotel

near a federal pen to interview
for a job I may not be well enough,
with my *preexisting condition,*
to accept, should it be offered,

I have to smile. How in hell
did you find me? Hearing the tenor,
pure Chianti, too eager to please,
I look up at you, old friend.

You seem remarkably fit — if
a bit smaller than life — for all
the years bruising our careers.
Seven Hills of Rome on the Korean TV.

O sole mio, and *Be my love,*
for no one else can end this yearning,
you'd croon from Father's 78s,
just the way Caruso taught you.

I heard you: *Listen kid, stand*
with arms out. Be a fighter. Let
even the cheapest seats know you
mean business. Chew the scenery

if you have to. No matter what,
make that grand final high C,
and don't for a moment forget where
it started, the neighborhood,

the blood. I knew she would—
the fair-skinned heroine,
elegant Wasp with Ivy lisp,
heavenly breasts and opal eyes

but cold as church at first—
eventually let herself come round,
slumping in your arms against
the tough muscle of your music,

an ethnic triumph great as garlic
and real bread, the two of you
and wild violins adding up to
a life, a story about America,

as Father, moist-eyed, saluted
the old record player, raising
his glass, "*Bravo, bravissimo,
Lanza.*" But there's more.

To entertain the Roman kids,
dressed for some neighborhood
between South Philly and Hollywood,
you begin to impersonate stars,

Perry Como, half asleep. Sinatra.
Then, brandishing the handkerchief,
Armstrong—Lanza doing Satchmo,
for Christ's sake! Wild applause

from us all, Roman urchins,
winter drummers and barflies,
cons in their unsnowy cells,
and I, who'd thought myself lost

at the dead end of the bar.
Memory can't lie too well,
you came by to remind, your notes
a kind of love. Good pipes—

only good, I'm not talking greatness
here—and a few tunes guarded
in the heart can see us through
the silences that riddle a life,

one night-fear we all come to,
that the body won't, finally,
live up to its billing, nor
will the soul. A voice so true

it can be thrown across the years
atones for many sins of wanting,
forgetting, calls us home again,
almost perfectly content.

The Beatification of Padre Pio

Pulses muffled in military underwear and medieval robes, rosaries clacking at their sides, the Sisters of Mercy passed photos down our fourth-grade rows. The eyes of a monk looked beyond, above us, lost utterly. I knew that, like my delicate piano teacher, he'd know nothing about baseball. But this was major league suffering. Sodden bandages swathed the hands. Blood and ache are as holy as it gets, we were told, blessings, grace, what we have in common with the bleeding god hanging on a tree, sung to and eaten each day.

Stigmata, a way belief disfigures the very fortunate. Greek for tattoo— puncture, prick of hot potsherd, pointed stick. Like Cain's fatal stain but enumerating divine wounds. Francis of Assisi invented it, as if dumb beasts, in their suffering at our hands, leave brands, draw blood. It trickles, seeps from wounds that don't heal, even in Paradise, from palms and feet, gushes out of the side to spray wildly like a dropped garden hose, amazing the centurion and the mother at the foot of the cross.

Stains remain where a murder occurs, crying out for more, which is the way God found pale Abel. This explains ages of bloodshed. Our mothers were made to believe this, the reason they cleaned and cleaned the house. After so many centuries, where on earth is there no blood? Whose hands are unstained? Everywhere, this animal rust.

Blood is the real miracle. The Italian crew testified that Padre Pio flew up to rescue them from the flaming, sputtering plane, a magic heart roaring like an engine, brown robe billowing out, the bright red on his hands and feet blinking, a beacon in the night.

Tarantella

Alone as anyone can be when,
a floor above, a mother taps
her foot, I'm seated on the bench
before cracked white keys,
discolored teeth of infinite minutes.
I don't yet know that nothing
is as true as the notes
and time signatures of childhood.
I study the drawing in the book,
the spider malevolent, leering,
the boy faint with fever.
His parents hold him up, force him
to sweat the poison out, dance away
from death. *Tarantella,* from *tarantula*—
as much as David dancing naked
and the Pied Piper, it made
its own sense, the spider, the tune,
the magic dance. Music the escape,
our sanctuary. It was years later,
belief having become a bad dream,
I read of tarantism, the Dancing Mania
of plague-time, penitents
jerked around by wild celestial music,
named for Taranto in the Italian South,
Greek Tarentum. It was the town
that named the tune, and even
the spider of sailor and crusader.
One day I brought my own sons,
not dancing but on a train and then
in a Ford Fiesta rented
from Hertz Italia, on a quest to hear
what Greek music remained
in southern Italy, and perhaps in us.
Time, this journey was about.
And music, of course.
This little dance and ditty
I'd been taught as a child,
and learned to be pure myth—

like nearly everything told me
by those older—proved later
to be so nearly true. I think
of Taranto ages ago, streets
filled with children whose parents
weep and clap and stamp their feet,
begging the young ones not
to stop, when knowing comes,
every damned and blessed memory.

> *The dark plague is nimble,*
> *my child. Never*
> *cease dancing.*
> *Don't disbelieve forever*
> *in everything we've sung*
> *you, just because*
> *we're stupid and foolish*
> *and of a slower time and world.*
> *Remember the words*
> *we found to make and keep you,*
> *heeds and family creeds*
> *in bass and treble clef,*
> *notes like steps*
> *that lead always away,*
> *always back to us.*

Quattrocento Angels over Cleveland

When I was new, I could believe angels
    commuted between the clouds
        and Cleveland,
    every tree and gutter brimming
with celestial song. A perfect pastel child and I
talked and sang on the way to school, and home again
    after the bell to do our chores,
        sat on the couch
    before TV, argued rules
of High Mass Latin, *Sorry!,* World War II.

My tiny guardian has expired, his older cousins—
    Powers, Dominions, Thrones—
        gone too,
    city jays and pigeons in their place.
Now I search for angels in quattrocento paintings,
sexual annunciations in the deep lapis and gold
    of Ionian sunset,
        perspective's sweep
    behind humans filthy rich or holy,
wonders running all the way to the vanishing point,

but discover only Fra Lippo Lippi's chubby imps
    mugging for the maestro,
        Botticelli's girls and boys
    languid or straight as pines,
Tuscan skies swallow-thronged. Even the highest art,
once the wealth it took is computed, disappoints,
    but we're suckers for cartoon promises,
        lies of the light,
    days unchanging *in saecula*
saeculorum, Amen. Our nighest dreams have wings.

Up we think is still the way to pray dark away,
     but *Thou shalt not to fly*
          is the commandment
     of this leaden world, bone stone-hard.
My body growing old in great and petty ways, nerves
like an old string of Christmas lights, the calendar
     riffling its pretty paintings,
          doves lamenting
     the fading city light,
I fear my angel has become my age.

Naming the Grandmother

The ancients believed
a name lives apart
from the person to whom
it is given. This I believe.

The Calabrian girl who sailed
in steerage from Platania
to Cleveland to make a boy
from Serrastretta

a man who would become
father of my father
is a skull full of auburn hair
atop a fine geometry

of bones old as anything
under cemetery grass
far beneath Ohio's winter,
far beyond any dream,

while *Carolina* remains
a flower glowing in my mind,
especially late at night
as I weed and prune

my highest memories
or move through the kitchen
fragrant with basil and garlic
in the gestures and steps

she taught me, old songs
flitting like spring birds through
my head. *Nonna. Nonna.*
Carolina Scarpino Citino.

IV. Walking the Mall

Hair

One by one the children,
large cartoon eyes shining,
push away from the table,
rise and walk away from us
into their rooms. Doors slam
hard. Loud music, the bass
throbbing deep in our teeth,
dark rooms of the heart.
Oooo Baby . . . Oooo Baby . . .
Years pass, time enough
for something grand,
something terrible to happen.
When they come out, our sons
have wild, unearthly voices.
Our daughter has budded, mastered
the art of embarrassment.
She won't look us in the eye.
Oh, Daddy, she says, corners
of her mouth turning down,
Oh, Daddy. And everywhere
there is hair. Such hair.

Cycladic Island Female Statue, British Museum

ca. 2500–2300 B.C.E.

Breasts lifted high by hands in offering,
so far from the arms-folded-across pose
of my daughter on cold days
or in front of the boys clumped
like hunters, pawing at the ground
with their Nikes, caps low over their eyes,
at Hastings Middle School—as if
she wished to conceal the form
of the woman she woke to find.
(Her new blood is another thing
she can't discuss with a father.)

Carved of smooth, moony white marble,
for this is all about living forever.
A dark delta signifies the pubis.
The blessing of then and now,
woman nearly too ancient and new.
Two circles and a triangle, oldest code,
what we once knew was worthy
of all worship, before the male gods came
with their stones for throwing,
sharp-barbed arrow-tips, long spears,
hard altars, their hateful, bristling angels.

The Puncture

Looking through the shoe boxes
of a life, lifting the stiff paper
where chemicals have caught
the light and the darkness
in which it swims, I'm pricked

by moments, times I wish
I'd been awake to the ache,
the joy breaking out inside
the frame. Now how they hurt—
Mother a thin-waisted bride,

breasts riding high. Father
all smiles, a second lieutenant
cocky and undemented,
home from Guadalcanal, ready
to get on with it. I sit here

on the floor, my grown children
spitting up on my shoulder,
wetting, mewling, my wife
in love unspeakably, reaching
back to unhook her bra,

eyes never leaving mine.
Roland Barthes argues
that in every photo that moves us
we find a spot of truth, a hook,
a sliver, a barb, the *punctum*—

an eye wound. Each shard
goes in hard or easy to raise
a spot, a spurt of red, to break
today's cluttered numb,
thick skin of habitude, to pierce

that place we used to call the soul.

Obsession

A sixteen-year-old boy obsessed with smelling nice died after months of repeatedly spraying his entire body with deodorant.
        AP

Nor can foot feel, being shod,
Hopkins says in "God's Grandeur."
How can nose know the real rose
from the faux? It's come to this.

Banks of foggers, each one large
as the screws of the *Titanic,*
turn our fields any odor we wish,
Vanilla Passion, Kiwi Apricot Musk

from the mall's Bath & Body Works.
My ninth-grade daughter, still
the angel who flew from heaven
between her mother's legs,

leaves for school smelling like nothing
found in nature. When no pines
are left, we can hang plastic trees
from the sides of glass malls,

just the right chemical soup
to dope our very noses
into not seeing clearly.
Back in the day, our tribe

made progress on all fours.
Now, we're too high to smell
where we've been, where
we're bound. *Your calf gods*

stink, O Samaria, Hosea
shouted at the unwashed crowd,
his face grave, wrinkled
in haughty distaste, a dried fig.

Time and again they whored
after sweet, beastly meat.
The prophet's God was lilac, wild-
flower, onion, new mown hay

drying in July fields. And then
you have the essence of love,
good sense we sucked in
at the breast. *I will come to you*

in two weeks, Napoleon, knowing
the sweet intensity of desire,
wrote to his dear Josephine.
Promise me you will not bathe.

Fecal Fossil Found

AP

We are so much less
than what we eat.
Most of a life's feast

we leave behind, day
by day, dusky earth
marking our fires,

smooth knucklebones
strewn like jewels
across dark routes

of beetle and worm—
so many precious relics
we've no use for.

What will I leave behind
of my last meal? Sated,
the tyrannosaur dropped this

65 million years ago,
"More than twice as big
as any previously reported

coprolite from a carnivore."
A life still steams.
This is hot. This is news.

Orange Beetle

Its shape has always epitomized for me the word *improbable*—maybe *goofy* as well. Not armadillo-like, exactly, having no tail; not an Inuit igloo, body heat keeping the occupants alive, though it came close to that on a few occasions, if I remember correctly; not quite a Roswell saucer, grown a tad fat and gaseous on New Mexican cuisine, this was an earthbound conveyance that recorded every bump in the road. Primitively modern, somehow, offering no immediate knowledge of whether it was coming or going, to tell the truth. We were a year past starting out, a married couple newly on the nest. No need, at long last, for a car to make love in (though we came awfully close at the drive-in a few times, out of habit, if memory serves me). We had rented a house, bought a bed (which was not much larger than the car) for that. The shape of the car we bought was the shape of my wife's new body, steeply sloped near and far in ways defying physics. I would usher, shoehorn her into the bright orange bug carefully, reverently. She was more precious than anything we'd ever come to own, we knew even then. And in time our first child rode in the back in a cardboard box fastened with the belt, until we bought a baby seat, our pretty, nearly hairless, portable puppy yipping and da-da-da-ing in back. My father had fought for the west side of Cleveland on Guadalcanal. Later, we'd have to secure his magnanimous victor's acceptance of every one of our Toyotas, until he mellowed in his last years and bought a Honda, but only because it was made in Ohio. He was Chianti-loud with praise for German engineers. He discounted the rumor he'd heard at the Ford dealership, that Hitler himself had designed this finless toy car. In those days we felt we owned all the time in the world, and then some. We drove an automobile that announced its owners as being young, happy to be cramped together on their way to some sort of eccentricity, but in no great hurry. These were mean Ohio streets down which our gaudy beetle skated, more orange than anything we could imagine. We were cold as bone in billows of windy white winter, frost blossoming on the windshield as we learned the dance of the tiny, reluctant clutch, lovers trying to make it to what comes next, baby stuff stowed in front. We bore our treasure proudly from place to place, our hot breaths inches from the flat, tiny windshield, the future chugging toward us like a lawn mower.

Horses *(for John Gabel)*

It is a remarkable fact that virtually all mammals
live an average of 1.5 billion heartbeats.
STEPHEN BUDIANSKY, *The Nature of the Horse*

Once I worshiped beasts so smooth,
touching them was a song, a pulse thrilling
up finger and arm, Trigger and Buttermilk
with unflowing manes, twitchless tails.
I'd put on the pliant plastic saddles, bridles,
take them off again. I didn't know then
counting means noting the passing
from our days of something precious,
paying attention for Roy and Dale,
the Sons of the Pioneers, and all the Indians.
We use up a thing so abundant and dear,
and we don't miss it until we miss it.
To live is to think not, remember
seldom enough. I've come this far,
Little Drummer Boy using up steps
with my *Rumpumpumpum*. Once,
horses were all our wealth. Their droppings
sweetened the soil of this republic.
The thunder of their hooves was music.
O where are they now, manes and tails,
proud, sleek necks of yesteryear,
brown muffins steaming under sun and stars,
those noble, fated, finite hearts?

Saying the Cold

How would you say *cold*
to one who'd never shivered—

and if, after years of sounding
it out, you found a way,

could you be heard as you'd need
to be? Want precedes language

as cold pleads for snow, the night
whistling through long bones

of the thigh, numb fingers, toes,
the piece of ice disappearing

slowly as it writes diminishing circles
around the breast of the lover

who had begged to be bound to the bed,
one nipple budding with need

nearly unspeakable, ache of teeth
and tongue, the moan so low. *Oh.*

Shoes

Magic, these little boats we sail, riding
perilous tides. "Nor can foot feel,
being shod," Hopkins claims,
but the bound foot feels too well
the torturer's whim, and what shoes

does God want on a woman? Not
the magic red ones that danced a girl
to death, nor the ruby slippers
that inflamed the green witch until,
aching to stroke the innocent sole,

she called Dorothy "My pretty."
I'd not understood these wonders
until you came breathless, bright-eyed
into the coffee shop where I'd
been waiting too long, growing

impatient, then angry. You said,
"Forgive me. I was making love
and lost all sense of time." Marriage
a dirty wind, your husband, the brute,
visiting his mother in Europe,

lover's wife at work, you told me
how, after the barefoot pas de deux
in their bed, fervent writhing
of dreamers blind to the damage
such tempests wreak, you'd gone

to the closet to see the clothes
of the woman whose man you'd fit
so well he'd shouted out "O God."
"A lovely woman," you said of the wife,
almost proudly, "Asian, lustrous hair,

a body so tiny that when I picked up
her shoes and placed my hands
inside, I filled them." And that act
of fondling, the violation of the shoes
with a hand damp with passion,

the taking of another's enchantment
was a possession greater than what
you'd done with her man,
Wicked Witch, you pulling the slippers
from the feet of the girl lying helpless,

unknowing on the storm-torn bed
and lost inside an alluring dream
that will turn out to be a lie,
rapt, holding your breath, slipping
long-nailed fingers into forbidden dark.

Dead Man Revives in Morgue

That it happened in Cairo
must mean something. Freud
says there are no accidents;
the newsgroup alt.conspiracy
and the Ohio Unorganized Militia
insist there is no coincidence.

The Egyptians know things about
the stony life beyond the grave.
They did for death and revivification
what the Japanese did for the auto —
made it a religion. Remember
those movie mummies summoned

to work Tut's curses, pretty girls
in tight skirts, blouses of an architecture
truly impressive, being toted off,
limp, to some dire fate, archaeologists
dying of fright or infarction —
and nearly also that little Ohio boy

in row 3, roll of NECCO wafers
sweating in his fist? Twelve hours
in the refrigerated morgue, and then,
brought back to consciousness,
finding the Other World a place
cold and dark as hell, yelling for help,

the newspaper *Al-Akhbar* reported.
It didn't say what he shouted, exactly,
but I can hazard a guess. Not,
certainly, the Egyptian version
of Twain's crack, *Reports of my death
have been greatly exaggerated.*

More likely something like *Hey,*
dammit! I'm not dead yet, or maybe,
afraid suddenly this really *is* death,
even though he can feel stainless steel
and smell refrigerant, wanting
to make his case, *God Is Great!*

Whatever, no one heard. When
the attendants arrived to remove
the body for the only rite
that ever really matters, burial,
and finally heard the knocking
and the cries, and finding him alive,

one of them collapsed in shock
and died. The staff of the morgue
waited hours for *his* call from the
refrigerated crypt, each one
praying not to be the one
to witness another cursed miracle.

When no call came, they locked
the icebox door just to be safe,
and went home, but none ever again
was able to sleep in peace,
just as, in the case of the current version
of that boy in the cinema, though

he likes to think himself wiser,
each night, on first lying down
in dark, remembering the years,
haunted by fears of God's curse and fire,
an eternity and a day of scream,
he would pray, *If I should die*

before I wake, Sweet Jesus, take
me to heaven, and, next morning,
though no longer able to pray,
he still wakes surprised,
elated enough to say, *Hey.*
I'm not dead yet. I'm not dead!

A Personal History of Sound, with Locomotive, Stage Murmurs, a Little Latin, a Little Sex

Let's start with a night,
so many to choose from,
but autumn or spring most likely,
pollen, spore your poison,
a sky oppressive with clouds,
change that chills mortally.

You hear faintly, as if
from far away, the news
that you can't breathe.
You must swallow, soon,
a bitter pill or burning mist
to make the noise, grown

closer now, cease. Confusion
sends you back to long
childhood asthma nights when
the precincts hissed
as you slept sitting up.
Mother smeared Vicks VapoRub

over your chest, a hand
icy across your nipples as
her eyes brimmed sorrow.
The pain it gave to think
you were making her
watch you expire, her boy,

a B&O locomotive straining
to yank wheezing cars
loaded with high-sulfur coal
into the Jones & Laughlin mill,
your mind loud as sex can be—
although what did you know then

of the antique wheeze of desire?
At last you grasp the inhaler
under jumbled coins and keys,
and you breathe, breathe in
with what space remains
in gripped, constricted bronchi,

and the cyanotic boy, befuddled,
slowly goes from blue to pink,
your kiss and all the fervor
you can muster sending him
back to the world. And yet
again, just last night,

in this your middle age,
before those assembled to hear
only you, an audience inspired
by each line, answering as if
your words inflamed tinder pews
of the Pentecostal church,

or maybe the "Murmur, murmur" when
there was need on stage
for the extras to make "Alarum."
You recall Father's line
to howling kids, "Keep it
down to a dull roar," and now

you're not given time
for even the briefest phrase,
as if altar boys answered
your *Dominus vobiscum* by shouts
of *Et cum spiritu tuo,*
and you're brought hard awake

to grating rales of your own chest
in labor, rousing you from a dream
of words so easy they sounded
like loud love, the light
raucous with dire music
of variable winds, the very air.

Walking the Mall

Young ones in their indolent hurry,
bare midriffs rippling, storm
toward me and away, jawing
about O.J., school, the big game.

On their way to lives they imagine
will be as flawless and grand
as their faces, legs, abs, they are
so lovely I could weep, here,

in the silvery nowhere of a mall
in Ohio, a state the tourist board
calls "The Heart of It All."
I'm walking because lesions

on my brain and spinal cord
make it hard, some days, to move,
even to think. I think about
these young, and the old who walk

with me because cold has driven
them here. It's so crowded today,
we're in the way, must keep
to the side, ceding right-of-way.

Youth looks through us into mirrors
positioned to show that looks
are everything, that life fascinates
only if we watch ourselves live.

As each young one passes a mirror,
he or she is joined in the glass
for an instant of eternity by one of us.
They, agile, fast on their feet,

can afford to study their perfection.
They don't need to watch where
they're going, while we,
battalions of the halt and old,

knowing how the future can rush
out of nowhere, look straight ahead,
away from mirrors, with admiration
and something like dread.

Sky Burial

1

Their Chinese overlords think it bizarre,
the dumb show of a slow, woeful race,
this setting out of the dead
like a village supper and summoning
the vultures. The old Tibetans, chafing
under the rifles of a foreign army,
say it's a way for the nothing
we become to float home,
begin over, rising on thermals
toward the hidden tops
of the last mountain. It has
everything to do, they say, with freedom.

2

There's no longer a need
for this fleshy shell, the body
having gone unsupple as shale.
The monk strips the flesh expertly,
as if he filleted a fish,
the knife sliding on the board
just above the skin beyond
the backbone. The inner organs
will make special treats, fit
for a gourmand, the fiercest,
most assiduous bird. He brings
the sledgehammer down
again and again, making morsels
of us, beak-sized, the bones
surprisingly fragile. We'd
been promised they'd last forever.

3

Just as the roots of a tree are said
to mirror the crown, a duplication
and balance below, above,
the dead flourish in numbers
that match the living.
At Calvary and Holy Cross
in Cleveland—where most
of my people have moved
to keep us living ones
from thinking too much
of ourselves—biding time
in the Earth Burial
we favor over here, we feed
the grubs, roly-poly bugs,
and of course, even children know
The worms crawl in, The worms
crawl out, The worms play pinochle
on your snout. Rather, we did
feed the earth once,
before stainless-steel caskets
and cement vaults, which seal in
the salt, bitter, sweet, and sour of us.

4

The Tibetans whose villages
are near a stream practice
Water Burial, where a body
is given as a gift to the fish.
Maddened by the lure and hook
of flesh, they plash and nibble,
mouthing a life away, gills
beating, a floating communion rite.
Now, this is *their* body.

5

When my spirit has left me,
I too would be a feast
for creatures of miracle
who breathe water or fly.
I will this body away.
It's already slowing, breaking out
in lesions of darkness eternal
along brain and spinal cord.
Already I can't feel the thistle seed
that fills my hands as I try to fill
the finch feeder. Already I need
to watch what I'm doing.
Come to me, grackle and finch,
starling, cardinal, and wren—
even you, vicious old crow, villain jay.
Stand beside the carrion me
in your feeding frenzy.
Poke and thrust and tear.
We'll rise above Ohio, light
as dawn, to begin the great migration,
and, when nature's run its course,
you'll drop me to earth to bless
the soil. In spring, I'll rise
from roots on tentative stems,
stand up in crowns of new green,
robes of carmine, ocher, blue.